www.finishinglinepress.com

Dirt

a poem by

Jennifer Handy

Finishing Line Press
Georgetown, Kentucky

Dirt

Publisher: Leah Huete de Maines
Editor: Christen Kincaid
Cover Art: Jennifer Handy
Author Photo: Jennifer Handy
Cover Design: Elizabeth Maines McCleavy

Order online: www.finishinglinepress.com
also available on amazon.com

Author inquiries and mail orders:
Finishing Line Press
PO Box 1626
Georgetown, Kentucky 40324
USA

Man is made of dirt—I saw him made. I am not made of dirt. Man is a museum of diseases, a home of impurities; he comes to-day and is gone tomorrow; he begins as dirt and departs as stench; I am of the aristocracy of the Imperishables. And man has the Moral Sense. You understand? He has the Moral Sense.

—Mark Twain

My parents sprang into existence at the ages
of 29 and 28. Before that
                    there was nothing;

I was not yet born. My mother might have been
a teacher, her subjects French and Spanish.
                    There might have been a marriage.

I know there was a ring. There were no wedding photos,
none I've ever seen. They might have gone to college
                    where they claim they never met,

though their college was the same, the same years
of attendance. But these weren't real events, not the kind
                    they talked about.

It's like saying the sky is blue and leaves are green.
They tell you that, maybe mention chlorophyll
                    and light waves, then pray to God

you shut your mouth. To ask questions is to pester,
which is to disobey your parents, which is
                    of course a sin.

I grew up in several houses in the suburbs, more than
two or three, houses with no front porches,
                    just a concrete stoop

to stand on so that the heels and wingtips and
patent leather stayed pristine on the way out
                    to the concrete driveway

or the mailbox. There were no back porches either,
though there were decks and patios, formal places
                    to house the propane grill

for cooking hot dogs in the summer and occasionally
for eating them at the outdoor table made of glass,
                                sitting on wrought iron chairs

on matching flowered upholstered cushions. But
more often we took the food inside, my parents
                                rejecting sunshine

and fresh air in favor of air conditioning.

When I was a little girl, before I learned that my mind,
my brain, was a computer that could perform
                    complex calculations

without the aid of feelings, I watched the Care Bears
on TV. I knew that real bears, the kind in nature,
                    a place I had heard of

but never been to, were not blue or green or pink.
They were black or brown or white, not real white
                    like drawing paper

or the Sheetrock on our walls, but yellowish,
discolored, like a toy that had been left outside
                    too many nights.

The bears in the zoo were like this. They were real.
I had seen them for myself. They had no emblems
                    on their bellies

and seemed to lack the special power of emanating
rainbows. These things I knew when I was four or five
                    and received a special gift.

I was over at my friend's house, we were playing
in her room when suddenly she took something,
                    I don't remember

what it was, perhaps a unicorn or a My Little Pony,
and she held it out to me and said that I could keep it.
                    I had never heard of this,

giving a gift outside of Christmas or a birthday,
where the gifts were all brand new, bought special
                    for the occasion.

But they weren't special really, I understood at once.
They had no meaning, no history, unlike this unicorn
                    that still had traces

of my friend upon it, the smudge of dirt upon its body,
the slightly tangled mane. And I knew then that we
                    were really friends.

When I took it home and showed it to my mother,
she was angry. She said I had to give it back.
                    Her parents had bought it

for her. It wasn't hers to give away.

In first grade I rode the school bus, which picked me up
right outside our mint green house. The other houses
                                built in the '70s

were also candy-colored in pastel shades.
One day on the bus I found a piece of candy
                                in my backpack.

It wasn't mine. I had no idea how it got there.
I can't remember whether or not I ate it.
                                The next day,

there was something different. A sparkly barrette.
Other things came later, nothing expensive
                                or very large,

just those little pieces of plastic that littered
childhood. These items posed a moral problem
                                because I knew

they didn't belong to me. If my mother found them
in my backpack, she would demand an explanation
                                and would expect me

to return them. I was sure she would not believe me
that I didn't know who they were from. So
                                I started sleuthing,

checking my backpack carefully at the end of school
each day. I checked again before I got off the bus.
                                That's when I always

found them. The last item was a marker in a shade
of reddish brown. My mother called them Magic Markers,
                                but this one was different.

Not Crayola, like all of mine, just some generic brand.
Right before I found the marker, I had turned my back
                    and caught a glimpse

of a girl named Candace who sat behind me with
her hand inside my bag. I asked her if she
                    had been the one

putting all these things inside my bag, and when
she didn't answer, just turned beet-red and nodded,
                    I noticed that she

was sitting all by herself. She was trying to buy
my friendship. So I told her that she could sit
                    with me and Tara.

Other forbidden things:
candy handed out from strangers, except of course on
	Halloween,
PG-13 movies,
Garbage Pail Kids, those trading cards that showed up
	at school and in the toy stores
	after the Cabbage Patch Kids came out
	and featured names like Slimy Sam
	and Run Down Rhoda. All
	the kids at school had them,
	everyone but me.
	When someone gave me one, my mother
	took it from me and threw it out like the garbage
	that it was.

Later, the forbidden list included
	R-rated movies,
	Dungeons & Dragons,
	fireworks, except the legal ones shot off on July 4th
		with parental supervision.

My parents were pioneers out in the Heartland,
talking about New York and California
                    as though they were foreign lands.

When I was seven, they packed up me and my little brother
and drove out several miles beyond the city limits
                    of Topeka, Kansas,

in our brand new station wagon, the kind with wood
along the sides. We went to unsettled territory,
                    a new development

next to Shawnee Lake, which my father said
was artificial, though it looked real enough to me.
                    We drove there first

to see the prep work for the foundation, the breaking
of virgin ground to make a walk-out basement.
                    My parents were beside themselves,

though my brother and I could not see why.
There was nothing there but dirt that had been
                    piled up and shifted.

From then on, we drove out every week or two
to check on the progress, to walk through the empty
                    skeleton, a frame

of two-by-fours that later were filled in with
insulation my father warned us not to touch,
                    that it was toxic.

We moved over the summer, making endless trips
in the station wagon with small loads of knickknacks,
                    dishes, kitchen items,

and other things my mother didn't want to pack, placing
the items in boxes with a few balls of wadded newspaper,
                    my mother driving

very slowly so as not to break her precious things.
For my brother and me, aged six and eight, the new house
                    was on the very edge

of the frontier. The little cul-de-sac was called
Tomahawk Court, and the house backed up to woods
                    which we named Greenwood Forest.

There was a creek that ran right through it, drainage
from the lake, which was on the other side.
                    The creek would freeze in winter,

and we were forbidden to ice skate on it,
though we did so anyway with just our tennis shoes
                    or snow boots on,

adventures that always ended when the ice broke
and one of us fell in. It wasn't deep enough to drown,
                    just deep enough

to soak a foot and leg, undeniable proof
of guilt. But the adventure I most remember
                    happened long before the winter,

right after we moved in. It was the final day
of summer, and my brother and I wandered over
                    to an empty lot

piled high with dirt, perhaps the very dirt dug out
from our own basement. We tried hard to shape it,
                    to tunnel through it,

to excavate a fort. But the loose dry dirt just crumbled,
refusing to stick together. There was no grass on it,
                    no roots to give the soil

any structure, just a few weeds here and there, mostly
thick stalks that grew spiky purple flowers.
                    Inside the stalks

we found a milky substance that we mixed in
with the dirt. We tore up the plants to extract it
                    but there wasn't enough

to turn the dirt into a clay-like substance
that back then we probably could only conceive of
                    as a natural form

of Play-Doh, and an inferior one at that.
At last, our mother called us in for dinner
                    and then a bath.

The next day would be my first at our new school,
and my brother's first day ever. He was starting
                    kindergarten, a funny word

that sounded like a kind of garden, a word adults
never explained except that it came before first grade.
                    That morning when I woke up

there was something very wrong with my eyes for I found
I couldn't see. I put hands up to my face, trying
                    to pry my eyelids open.

Suddenly, a little slit of my bedroom
came into focus. I walked over to my dresser,
                    to the mirror,

where I inspected my other eye, which still
refused to open. I ran down to my parents' bedroom—
                    my father had left already—

and woke up my mother, crying, half hysterical,
telling her I couldn't see, I had gone blind,
                    my eye was shut or glued

or something. She got up and saw immediately
what I, in my frantic state, had missed: my whole face
                    was red and puffy,

one eye swollen shut entirely, the other
just barely open. It must have been that milkweed
                    you were playing with,

she said, you must be allergic. I didn't know
that it was milkweed, that even weeds had names.

The new school was named Tecumseh South, which was
a Native American name. The Tecumseh Indians.
                    Our mascot was a mustang,

some type of horse related to the Indians, I imagined,
in the same way that a unicorn is related
                    to little girls.

We studied the Native Americans each Thanksgiving
by making headdresses out of feathers, though back then
                    we always called them Indians.

Shawnee Lake was practically in our backyard, and
the high school teams were the Thunderbirds, which
                    I also recognized as being

vaguely Indian, the Thunderbird logo looking
like something straight off a totem pole. No one
                    spoke much about these things,

except the Trail of Tears, which was supposed
to make us cry, except it didn't. I cried
                    only later at the movies

when I saw *Dances with Wolves*, a movie featuring
the frontier, tee-pees, buffalo, and a white man.

At least once a year, my family ventured out of Kansas.
There was our summer vacation, for one thing,
                    and the trips to Oklahoma

to watch a college football game at my parents'
alma mater, a word that meant their college,
                    which was OU,

the home, as my parents informed us over and over,
of the Sooner Schooner, a covered wagon
                    pulled by two horses

named Boomer and Sooner, a wagon that pranced
around the field to the tune of "Boomer Sooner."

          I was Sooner born and Sooner bred
          and when I die I'll be Sooner dead.

Throughout the trip to Norman, my parents broke out
into a rousing rendition of this chorus
                    singing it as though

it were the only song that mattered. They didn't
tell us about their college days. They reminisced
                    instead about The Boomerang,

a local burger stand turned restaurant. I didn't realize
at the time the OU connection in the name.
                    I thought it was Australian.

My parents went on frequent trips to exotic lands
around the world: Jamaica and Hawai'i,
                    Thailand and New Zealand,

Hong Kong, China, and Australia. My brother and I
stayed home with babysitters. When they came back,
                    they brought us souvenirs:

carved coconuts, jade necklaces, stuffed animals
made from real kangaroo fur, woven baskets,
                    a boomerang,

silk pajamas, a didgeridoo, a painting
of the Sydney Opera House. These were the tokens,
                    our living proof,

of a greater outside world. As for us, our parents
kept our family vacations to places that boasted
                    a Six Flags or Disneyland.

A trip to Epcot Center was our first exposure
to other countries, where I bought a German bear,
                    which was brown, the way

a bear should be. I named him Hermann after his maker,
the German company. I knew no other German names,
                    though my mother's father

probably was German. He was supposed to be
my grandfather, but he was dead, a ghost, and could hardly
                    be expected to fill the role.

As we toured through what passed for Europe, a simulated land,
my mother didn't talk about her summer there,
                    except her oft-repeated

comment about how much she liked the Louvre.
She never mentioned a single painting.

My father's company, the only one he worked for,
cut down hardwood trees across the continental
                    United States, turning

the old-growth forests into two-by-fours and other
building products used to make the modern houses
                    and shopping centers

that forever creep not only westward, but north
and east and south, out from every city, along every
                    interstate and freeway.

When we watched our house go up, I remember
seeing the blue Georgia-Pacific logo printed,
                    over and over,

across the house before the wood siding covered it up,
hiding its existence to everyone who wasn't there,
                    who didn't see it built,

who didn't know the specific layers that lay
beneath the paint. When we left that house less than five years later,
                    I didn't know it then,

but I would never live in another house whose innards
I had inspected as a witness to its creation.
                    Our next house wasn't made

of wood at all, but the Acme brick that's all over Texas,
a product advertised back then by Troy Aiken,
                    a football player,

and famous, my parents told me. We saw him once
in Dallas at a fancy restaurant before a concert.
                    He was wearing a tuxedo,

and my parents whispered about him, about the Cowboys,
but all I could think of was Acme brick.
                        I went to junior high

in Texas, where I finally got to choose my classes.
I was required to choose a foreign language,
                        something I dreaded taking.

I never did believe that I could speak words
from somewhere else, from other people, and so
                        I signed up for Latin,

a dead language, one I wouldn't have to speak.
I had a French name from my mother, and though she
sometimes
                        sang "Frère Jacques,"

she didn't teach me any French. No Spanish either.
When I asked her about this later, she claimed
                        "Oh, you just weren't interested."

She didn't teach my brother either, and he signed up
for German.

Things I learned too late,
when they were no longer relevant:
        Lake Shawnee was a Depression era make-work project.

        There are no Tecumseh Indians.
        They are not a nation
        or a tribe, though there was a famous chief of the Shawnee
        named Tecumseh, an opponent of white expansion.

        There was once a baseball team
        named the Tecumseh Indians. Minor league. Defunct.
        The team was in Tecumseh, Michigan.
        They never played in Kansas.

        My mother's favorite brands,
        Brawny and Quilted Northern,
        were both Georgia-Pacific products.

The only Spanish words I knew while growing up
        were *Pablo*, the Spanish version of my father's name,
        and *casa*, which I may have been confused about,
                        thinking it meant restaurant
                        or maybe kitchen since it was in all
                        the Tex-Mex restaurant names.

I was in my twenties before I realized
I couldn't say hello in French or Spanish,
and that my mother had sung "Frère Jacques"
almost exclusively in English.

        Are you sleeping? Are you sleeping?
        Brother John? Brother John?
        Morning bells are ringing, Morning bells are ringing.
        Ding ding dong. Ding ding dong.

        Frère Jacques, Frère Jacques . . .
The rest she only hummed.

The one thing my mother told me about their trip
to Thailand was that the place
was positively filthy,
that you couldn't pay her to go back there.

About China, she reported that the government
was corrupt, that the state
of the panda bears in the Beijing zoo
was awful. Their fur, she said, was so dirty
they didn't look black and white,
but rather black and brown.

And much later, when I pressed her,
she would confess
that she didn't like OU at all,
not when she was there.

When we first moved to Texas,
there were no Hispanic people in our neighborhood,
but there was a single black family down the street from us.
My mother said she thought it would be good for us kids
to meet them, but looking back,
I remember only a casual wave.
I don't recall saying hello to them even once,
not in any language.

I went to college in Oklahoma, but not OU.
By then, my parents had left Texas and lived
                    in an almost identical

suburb outside of Denver. I lived in a dorm, where
my father claims, my grandmother once lived.
                    She died when I was five,

but my parents wouldn't let me attend the funeral.
If I had learned "Frère Jacques" in French,
                    I might have known

that the root word for dormitory meant sleep,
something I didn't realize even in French class,
                    which I took my freshman year,

back when "freshman" wasn't a sexist word.
The landscape I grew up in admitted no logic,
                    no etymology,

no history. Just a collection of facts without meaning,
a dictionary where all the words are unrelated.
                    And so it came

as no surprise, when I asked to be allowed to go
abroad for a five-week course in France, that my mother
                    was the one to say

that no, I couldn't go. I spent the summer term
at home. As if in compensation, my mother
                    finally told me something

about her father. She told me he was a butcher,
and she told me his first name. But it turned out
                    these things have limits,

certain timeframes, because I soon forgot the name.
He had existed too long in my mind
                        as a nameless, faceless man,

and the name, whatever it was, seemed wrong and foreign,
so like a Post-it note, its adhesive slowly weakened
                        until at last it dropped away.

It could have been Hans or Frank or Frederick. I never thought
to ask again. When I went back to school, I met a girl
                        not from Oklahoma

who was astounded by the dirt. If you've never
seen it, it's a distinctive shade of reddish brown.
                        I went with her

to Lake Thunderbird one weekend, where she
collected a mason jar of it to take back home
                        to prove to everyone

in South Dakota that some dirt is really red,
even if it isn't quite as red as blood.
                        But I wondered even then

if maybe there was something more, if maybe
she was going to keep that jar of earth as some kind
                        of souvenir.

After college, I didn't go back home. There was
no home really to go back to. I trekked out
                    to California,

though I didn't go by covered wagon, nor by car.
I sold my stuff and moved by plane, watching
                    the squares of earth

upon the plains, the perfectly shaped fields, turn into
vast tracts of mostly uncultivated desert land.
                    In California,

I taught English, often to students whose first language
was something else. I married an attorney
                    whose clients were Hispanic.

We visited the Spanish mission in San Francisco,
the place that gives the name to the Mission District.
                    It's free to go there

except for the suggested donation, which is enforced
with harsh words and looks. There's a beautiful garden
                    there, the one that's in

that Hitchcock movie *Vertigo*. There are gardens
throughout San Francisco, a city made of stucco,
                    stone, and money.

I loved that city until we moved there,
and I saw what money really meant, when
                    there's never enough of it,

when people move in and out every month,
every day, when people move out onto the street.
                    Like so many others,

we moved out to the suburbs, where there were shootings on BART and on the freeways. The distance is enraging, this sense that you are

too far away from where it is you want to be.

The wild land we bought some five years later
was in Northern California, just on the border
                          of Oregon.

My parents were visiting us when we closed,
my husband dashing off furtively with the laptop
                          to make sure it all went through.

I hadn't told my parents we were buying it,
this undeveloped plot of land, 40 acres
                          with no house or well

or running water, just trees and springs and natural pasture,
grass that grows five feet tall in summer. In one direction,
                          mountains, in the other,

a shallow lake that, when it isn't dry,
reflects the setting sun. I hadn't told them
                          we planned to move there,

to build some kind of better life. I remember
when my father used to talk of hippies,
                          environmentalists,

tree-huggers, he always called them, and he found them
ridiculous. But I remembered Greenwood Forest,
                          though I knew almost nothing

about it, only the name of a single tree, the dogwood,
a tree with two- and three-inch thorns that we always
                          tried to stay away from.

There was another kind of tree with deep purple berries
that grew over by Shawnee Lake. I used to eat them,
                          the berries, though I knew

I shouldn't. They could be poisonous, but they glistened
in the sun. Surely something so beautiful would never
harm me. And so I tried one.

I ate a few at first, and when I didn't die,
I went back the next day and ate some more.
They were the most delicious

fruit I'd ever tasted. Decades later, I discovered
almost by accident they were mulberries.
There were some berries

on our land. I looked up what colors tended
to be poisonous and avoided those. I sampled
the others, the ones

the black bears ate, assuming they weren't toxic,
but they were sour. Later we could plant an orchard,
and we bought an apple tree

that promptly died. But the first thing was a structure.
When I said the land was empty, that wasn't really true.
The previous owner

had started building a structure on it, a giant platform
with three walls and a roof that jutted out to cover
a pull-through space

for a camper or RV. The exterior wasn't finished.
He had started to lay stones, ones gathered from the land,
up the sides, but he hadn't

gotten far, not more than three feet in most places,
and the walls were at least sixteen feet high.
There was a cut-out frame

for a door and several others for windows,
but these were not installed, and the rest of the interior
                        was simply two-by-fours

without drywall or insulation. A fourth wall
had never been intended, or so it seemed to us.
                        I had a vision

of finishing this place, leaving the front part
open to look out over the lake. But my husband
                        vetoed that, arguing

that zero degrees requires walls, even if
they're made of canvas, which is what we settled on.
                        We set up a wall tent

complete with wood-burning stove. That first winter,
we would light a fire to raise the temperature
                        before changing

into pajamas, all wool, several layers, two pairs of socks,
turtlenecks, mittens, wool stocking caps. As the fire died down,
                        we crawled onto our mattress

made of straw, covered with wool blankets and a sheepskin rug,
and snuggled together, tightly tucking the blankets
                        around our bodies

to keep the heat in. At night, the snow fell gently
all around and on our tent. We could hear the owls
                        and the coyotes

and other wild noises we never could identify.
It was romantic, getting up at sunrise,
                        going out into a world

glittering with ice to cook over an open fire.
I tried to convey this to my parents, though they
                    didn't seem to comprehend.

My father told me one day on the phone,
you know your great-grandparents lived in a dugout
                    when they were settlers

in Oklahoma before they built their house.
He said it offhandedly as though it were a factoid
                    gleaned from Wikipedia.

I didn't tell him about the problems on the land,
problems that were growing, just like the piles
                    of trash and garbage.

Things scattered across our land:
        Quaint wooden buckets lined with paraffin
        that cracked that first December,
        no longer water-tight,
        but wet from snow and growing moldy.

        A twenty-gallon cast-iron vessel
        called a potje meant to boil large amounts of water,
        but too big to manage or to move
        out of the fire-pit, away from the snow
        that made it rust.

        A tent that weighed a hundred pounds with zippers
        that happened to leak profusely around the doors
        at the bottom, where the snow was.

        A tent stove that smoked so much it made us cough
        and all the tent pipes that fit into it,
        pipes that were too large
        for the second stove we finally bought.

        Perhaps a thousand empty water bottles,
                gallon-sized,
        that could only be recycled in California,
        when it just so happened
        that the closest town to us by far was in Oregon.

        Endless clumps of bleached-white toilet paper which,
                as it turned out,
        was extremely slow to compost.

        An empty beehive bought too late
        in the season to order any bees.

        A bus full of furniture
        that I hoped one day to use again,
        barrister bookcases,

Art Deco dressers,
even a piano, sadly out of tune thanks to the
moisture and the weather.

Twelve-foot-long pieces of green plastic roofing
from the unfinished platform structure.

Decaying nails
and portions of rusty screen
from what appeared to be a dilapidated cabin,
a relic of some forgotten past,
unknown,
unknowable.

Our driveway was more than half a mile long
and made of dirt that, in the winter snows,
                    turned straight to mud.

We had to use tire chains six months of the year
just to pick up mail and groceries. The driveway
                    ran first over federal land

before it wound its way to ours. There was a sign,
a historical marker, indicating that the road,
                    our driveway,

was once part of the Oregon Trail, an obscure
California branch. The land was in Modoc County,
                    home of the Modoc people,

a small group of Native Americans that put up
an extended campaign against white encroachment
                    during the Modoc War.

They lost the war, but they put up a damn good bloody fight.
There are books about it in the local libraries,
                    and books about native plants,

the juniper, pines, and sagebrush that grow wild
at 5,000 feet in elevation across high desert land.
                    I know more about this land

than anywhere else I've ever lived, including Kansas,
where I took the required class in state history.
                    Still, my knowledge

is fragmented, temporary, written only
so deep, like footprints in snow or mud.
                    We don't know how to fish,

our fishing pole lying untouched, unused,
how to grow apples successfully, how to remove the algae
                    from the spring and clean the water

well enough for drinking, how to make a tent last
more than a single year, how to construct a platform
                    for a canvas yurt

or some other more permanent form of housing,
how to string up barbed wire to patch the fence
                    to keep in sheep for milk

and mutton, how to build a chicken coop, the best place
to plant a garden without an expensive greenhouse,
                    how to hunt wild deer

for venison, how to tan the skins into leather,
how to repair boot soles that quickly degenerate
                    when worn daily on rocky land,

how to deal with a swarm of a hundred wasps
inside our tent without resorting to pesticides,
                    how to live upon the land

without spending more money than we have to do it.
Any one thing we could learn, but we need to know
                    everything all at once.

We take things one day at a time, trying to ignore
the trash as it piles up around us. Eventually,
                    we can't ignore it,

that we don't know how to live or what to do,
so one day we just take off and leave it all behind.
                    I am my parents' child.

No bit of earth is sacred.

Jennifer Handy is the author of the poetry chapbooks *California Burning* (Bottlecap Press, 2024) and *Dirt* (Finishing Line Press, 2025). She is the recipient of a Pearl Hogrefe Fellowship for poetry. Her poetry has been published in *The Ilanot Review, Interim, Watershed Review, Voices,* and elsewhere. She was longlisted in the 2024 Frontier Poetry Nature & Place Prize and received the Honorable Mention in the Wil Mills Chapbook Award contest at West Chester University.

www.ingramcontent.com/pod-product-compliance
Lightning Source LLC
Chambersburg PA
CBHW022055080426
42734CB00009B/1360